HOW TO
KNOW
YOU'RE
SAVED

HOW TO KNOW YOU'RE SAVED

C. Donald Cole

Moody Publishers

Chicago

© 1988, 2008 by
C. DONALD COLE

Cover Design: John Hamilton Design (www.johnhamiltondesign.com)
Cover Image: Barry Rosenthal / Getty
Interior Design: Ragont Design

Library of Congress Cataloging-in-Publication Data
Cole, C. Donald.
    How to know you're saved / by C. Donald Cole.
        p. cm.
    ISBN-13: 978-0-8024-3632-0
    ISBN 10: 0-8024-3632-3
    1. Assurance (Theology) 2. Salvation—Christianity. I. Title.

BT752.C65 2008
234—dc22
                                                        2008003653

We hope you enjoy this book from Moody Publishers. Our goal is to provide high-quality, thought-provoking books and products that connect truth to your real needs and challenges. For more information on other books and products written and produced from a biblical perspective, go to www.moodypublishers.com or write to:

Moody Publishers
820 N. LaSalle Boulevard
Chicago, IL 60610

3 5 7 9 10 8 6 4 2

This booklet is dedicated to Christians who lack assurance
but, like those noble people of ancient Berea,
are willing to search the Scriptures
to find out that they can be saved and know it

CONTENTS

INTRODUCTION

*I*n 1971 I became the host of the radio program *Dial the Pastor*. The program was broadcast from the studios of the Moody Bible Institute in Chicago. At that time, reception was limited to the area covered by WMBI's transmitter, mainly eastern Illinois and northwestern Indiana. Even so, the potential number of listeners was enormous. Listeners were invited to call and ask questions about the Bible. What does the Bible say, what does it mean, and how can it be applied to life today? It was never necessary to wait for a call.

Most listeners to Christian radio stations are believers. Perhaps surprisingly, they represent the whole spectrum of Christian tradition—from older denominations to the latest independent group. As might be expected, they often disagree about peripheral issues. In fact, they may not even agree as to what are the peripheral issues! They are alike, however, in that they subscribe to the truths set forth in the great creedal statements of the historic church, such as the Apostles' Creed.

They are also alike in that they want to know how the Bible answers questions not handled in the historic creeds. What does the Bible teach about baptism? What does it say about church polity? Who was Cain's wife? Does the Bible permit divorce and remarriage? Will we know each other in heaven? Will those who die in childhood be children forever? The creeds don't handle questions such as these. On *Dial the Pastor* I did—although not always successfully.

Later, with the development of a satellite network, *Dial the Pastor* became part of the nightly program *Open Line*, broadcast nationally. I wondered if listeners outside the WMBI listening area would ask different questions about the Bible and Christian living. Now I know the answer. Believers around the country are troubled by, or curious about, the same things. But of all the serious questions that Christians ask, what is the most common?

Christians want to know if they can be certain of heaven. They want to know whether they can be saved and *know for certain that they are saved*. In other words, can one have positive, unshakable assurance of salvation? Or is it possible to lose one's salvation? This question vexes more believers than any other. And this is the question this booklet undertakes to answer.

Why do sincere Christians lack assurance of salvation? Why do they worry about the possibility that they may lose their salvation? First, they have inadequate knowledge of the *basis* of salvation (they don't understand the meaning of the cross). Second, they have inadequate knowledge of the *way* of the salvation (they don't understand the meaning of faith and God's part in saving us). Third, they have misconceptions about the *results* of salvation (they expect perfection and don't understand sin in their lives after conversion).

Sometimes a fourth reason for lack of assurance of salvation is deliberate, persistent sin in a believer's life. Fear of loss of salvation is inevitable in a person who persists in doing what he knows is wrong.

This booklet is an attempt to reassure Christians that, having been truly saved, they can no more lose their salvation than God can lie. However, having salvation as an eternal possession is one thing; knowing for certain that one has it is something else. Sinners are saved when they accept salvation according to God's terms. They can have assurance (i.e., *confidence*) that they are eternally saved only to the extent that they *understand* the way of salvation and *believe* it.

While assurance depends in part on subjective factors, knowledge and understanding of the Word of God are essential to it. That's the reason for this booklet. Its purpose is to instruct—and by instructing to reassure.

One

The Basis of
SALVATION
*How a holy God can save
sinful people and still be holy*

*I*n eighteen years of preaching the gospel in Angola, I never met an African believer who was certain of his or her salvation. No matter how firm these believers' faith in Jesus, they seemed incapable of complete assurance. In their opinion, it was presumptuous to believe that they could or would hold fast to God. The best a believer could do, they thought, was *hope* that he or she would be believing at the moment of death and, therefore, go to heaven.

Does that sound familiar? That is the position of many sincere Christians. They combine genuine faith in God through Christ with lingering fear that they might miss heaven after all. They *hope* that they will be true to the end and qualified to pass through the gates of heaven. But they're not sure.

In every case, whether in Angola or the United States or anywhere else, that troubling uncertainty arises from an inadequate understanding of the basis of salvation. On what grounds does

God save us? How is it possible for a holy God to save unholy
people without compromising His character? In other words, is
there a solid biblical basis for salvation? If so, what is it?

The basis of salvation is, quite simply, the cross of Christ.
What, then, is the cross? The cross was an event, and the cross *is* a
symbol. Viewed as an event, the cross was an episode in history.
Jesus Christ was put to death on a cross. Viewed as a symbol, the
cross stands both for the death itself and *its meaning* as set forth in
Scripture. The cross is the supreme symbol of Christianity—the
basis of our hope.

The historic creeds of Christendom emphasize the importance of the cross. For example, the cross is the heart of the Apostles' Creed:

> I believe in God the Father Almighty, maker of heaven and
> earth: and in Jesus Christ, His only Son, our Lord, who was
> conceived by the Holy Ghost, born of the virgin Mary, suf-
> fered under Pontius Pilate, was crucified, dead, and buried:
> He descended to hell; the third day He rose from the dead; He
> ascended into heaven, and sitteth on the right hand of God the
> Father Almighty; from thence He shall come to judge the
> quick and the dead.

Only three words in the Apostles' Creed make direct reference
to the cross as an event: "suffered" and "was crucified." Everything that follows—"dead," "buried," "descended," "rose,"
"ascended," "sitteth," and "shall come to judge"—contributes to

the meaning of the cross. For example, if Christ had not risen from the dead, His death would have been an ordinary death—and therefore meaningless. His rising invests His death with profound meaning.

The Creed says nothing, however, of Christ's life. That holy life is not an object of belief but of emulation. The main event in Christ's life was His death, and by linking His sufferings with Pilate, the Creed both fixes the time of Christ's death and underscores its historicity. Christ's death was an event in time, and the secular world is forced to confirm it. If the cross is mentioned in secular circles, educated listeners think immediately of the crucifixion of Jesus Christ under Pontius Pilate.

WHY CHRIST DIED

If the cross is mentioned in Christian circles, most listeners think about the meaning of Christ's death. The crucial question is, Why did He die? Nowhere is this aspect of Christ's death more clearly stated than in Romans 4:25 ("He was delivered over to death for our sins") and Romans 5:8 ("While we were still sinners, Christ died for us"). Therefore the answer to the question is that He died for us, for our sins.

Theologians usually express this truth by saying that Christ's death was *vicarious*, meaning that He died as a substitute for sinners—in other words, He died in our place. This answers the question Why did He die? but raises at least two other questions. First, Why did we need a substitute? And second, Why was it necessary that Christ be that substitute?

The answer to the first question is sin—human sin, which brought all humanity under the sentence of death and the judgment of God. Alone we could not survive God's wrath concerning our sin. If there were no substitute, if we had nothing to offer God but the usual excuses for sin, we would perish eternally—in hell. God's wrath would rest on us forever. We need a worthy substitute—someone who can stand in our place and endure God's wrath for us so that we need not endure it.

The answer to the second question is closely related to the first. Jesus Christ needed to be that substitute because He alone was worthy. He alone was sinless and, therefore, exempt from the universal sentence of death. So, if He would die voluntarily, His death *could* be vicarious—if that was His intention and if God agreed. He could have died in somebody's place. And that is exactly what He did.

Furthermore, because He was more than a man (He was divine), His death had infinite value. "Infinite" means that by dying He became the substitute for an *unlimited* number of persons. He died for the whole world, including you and me.

In addition, the *way* Christ died is important. He didn't die in bed; He died on a cross—as the Old Testament predicted in passages such as Psalm 22:16: "They have pierced my hands and my feet." The significance of death by crucifixion is made clear in Deuteronomy 21:23: "Anyone who is hung on a tree is under God's curse." That text explains in part the horror Jews felt when told that Jesus was the Messiah. In their minds, that their Messiah would be crucified was unthinkable. A crucified person was under

God's curse. But that, Paul told believers in Galatia, is the point. By dying on the cross, "Christ redeemed us from the curse of the Law, having become a curse for us—for it is written, 'Cursed is everyone who hangs on a tree'" (Galatians 3:13 NASB).

Clearly, the manner in which Christ died is theologically significant. By hanging on a cross (tree), He took upon Himself the curse of God. He was treated by God as if He were accursed, as if He were under the curse of God's law, even as if He were sin itself. The curse of the law (that is, the lethal consequences of sin, which were proclaimed in the law) was shifted from us to Him. By dying He removed the curse from those who trust Him. Now the law has no further claims against sinners who trust Jesus; it no longer pronounces a sentence of eternal death against them. As an unknown hymn writer expressed it,

> *Whatever curse was mine, He bore,*
> *The wormwood and the gall;*
> *There, in that lone, mysterious hour,*
> *My cup—He drained it all!*

GOD'S ROLE IN CHRIST'S DEATH

Where was God when Jesus suffered and died? This is the crucial question, because if God was just a bystander, assurance of salvation is impossible. Assurance of salvation is impossible without assurance that God was involved in all that Christ did—from Mary's womb to Joseph's tomb.

God was *there*, at the cross—overseeing a death that He Himself had planned before the foundations of the earth were laid. In speeches to the citizens of Jerusalem, Peter accused them of handing Jesus over to wicked men to be crucified. Peter explained, however, that Christ's death was the fulfillment of a plan that God had announced through the prophets. It was according to "God's set purpose and foreknowledge" (Acts 2:23; cf. 3:18). Thus, God had been there all the time; no matter how disordered events seem to have been, God was in control.

That is not to say that God wrote the play and moved people around like puppets. God doesn't tempt or coerce people into doing evil. He fulfills His plans by bringing to power those whose inclinations lead them to do the things that accomplish divine purposes. What this means, among other things, is that the cross was not merely a monstrous mistake. It was an accomplishment of enormous significance. On the Mount of Transfiguration, Moses and Elijah appeared with Jesus, "speaking of His departure which He was about to bring to accomplish at Jerusalem" (Luke 9:31 NASB). His death was an achievement.

This point is terribly important. Assurance of salvation depends on our understanding that God was personally involved in Christ's death *and* that His death—and His death alone—is the basis of salvation. Assurance of salvation is impossible for those who believe that something else is required. If, for example, great faith is required, how can anyone know that his faith is strong enough? And if good works are required for salvation, how can anyone know for certain that he has done *everything* necessary?

Was God really involved in the cross, or was He just a spectator? Paul's answer is plain. Paul says in 2 Corinthians 5:19–21,

> *God was in Christ personally reconciling the world to himself—not counting their sins against them—and has commissioned us with the message of reconciliation. . . . For God caused Christ, who himself knew nothing of sin, actually to be sin for our sakes, so that in Christ we might be made good with the goodness of God.* (PHILLIPS, emphasis added)

God was not "in" Christ in the sense that He is "in" us who believe. The sentence should be punctuated to indicate that through Christ—who, though one with the Father, was nonetheless distinct from Him—God was enabled to accomplish His purpose. Thus the sentence should read, "God was, in Christ, personally reconciling the world to Himself." God was most definitely involved in the cross—not as a small-time player but as the major participant. He produced and directed the play, so to speak. Thus, the cross was a divine production—God and Christ acting in concert to be able to offer reconciliation to a lost world.

Substitution

The statement that Christ "knew nothing of sin" has bearing on the rich meaning of the cross. An innocent victim was crucified. Jesus had no personal experience of sin. No evil thoughts existed in His heart, no bad words in His mouth, no wrong actions at any time. Hence, He was not under the sentence of death; He didn't have to die, as we do, because of personal sin. Therefore His death—which was voluntary—was different; it was vicarious, or substitutionary. He died in our place for our benefit.

Christ died also for God's benefit, although in an entirely different sense. Christ's death gave God a satisfactory basis for exercising mercy. God can now save us, not because we deserve salvation or because He decides to overlook sin, but because Christ's death satisfied the demands of God's holiness. God demands death as the penalty for sin. Christ paid that penalty *as God intended that He should.* That is what Jesus meant when He rebuked Peter in Gethsemane: "Shall I not drink the cup the Father has given me?" (John 18:11). The "cup" was a figure of speech, meaning His sufferings unto death. Jesus took the cup from His Father's hand and, by dying, satisfied all that God required.

Propitiation

This is the meaning of that great biblical word *propitiation.* That word is not generally part of our everyday vocabulary; consequently, some modern Bible translations drop the word, using "sacrifice of atonement" or something similar. That is a pity. Some words, including "propitiation," are required to represent the concept the writer wishes to present. To learn the meaning of some Bible words may take a little effort, but it's worth it. Other studies and disciplines also require the learning of special words. No one expects the legal profession to rewrite its texts in simple English. Law students have to master new words if they wish to be lawyers. Why should any less be expected of people who are serious about Bible study?

Paul uses the word *propitiation* in one of the richest passages in the New Testament. Paul said, "Christ Jesus; whom God displayed publicly as a propitiation" (Romans 3:25 NASB). John uses the word twice:

If anyone sins, we have an Advocate with the Father, Jesus Christ the righteous; and He Himself is the propitiation for our sins. (1 John 2:1–2 NASB)

In this is love, not that we loved God, but that He loved us and sent His Son to be the propitiation for our sins. (1 John 4:10 NASB)

As used in the Bible, "propitiation" means Christ, by dying, took the full force of God's wrath against sin and so enabled God to look on us with favor. In other words, Jesus satisfied the death penalty for our sin, so that we don't have to. He died in our place. Christ's death freed God to do what He wanted to do—save sinners—but could not have done without compromising His holiness. Christ's death, a propitiation (or satisfaction of the death penalty), provides a righteous basis for a holy God to save sinners.

That is how Paul explains the propitiatory character of Christ's death. It demonstrates God's righteousness. It shows that God does not turn a blind eye to sin. His wrath against sin demanded that its penalty be paid in full, and it *was* paid in full—at the cross. Now, having been propitiated (satisfied) by the death of His Son, God is able to save sinners.

Christ's death was for God's benefit; it enabled Him to turn His wrath away from its natural objects—sinful people. Christ's death as a propitiation provides a meeting place for a holy God and sinful people.

God is propitiated; His character is vindicated; and sinful people are invited to draw near and be forgiven.

By dying, Christ endured God's wrath against sin. God's wrath is both His attitude of hostility toward sin and His determination to avenge or punish sin. Christ endured God's wrath by accepting responsibility for our sins and suffering the consequences on the cross. Paul said that "God made him who had no sin to be sin for us" (2 Corinthians 5:21). God and Christ acted in concert. Jesus willingly accepted responsibility for our sins. He did not become sin in the sense of committing sin, because He was at all times personally sinless. Nevertheless, God *treated* Him as if He were sin and dealt with Him as if He were the scapegoat for the entire universe.

Was the cross a miscarriage of justice? Yes, in one respect it was, because Jesus in no way deserved it. Yet at its deepest level, the cross was a manifestation of purest justice. Christ had agreed to come to the earth to be the Savior of the world. Yet He could not save the world except by assuming responsibility for the world's sins. Having assumed that responsibility, He could not escape God's wrath against sin. God's holiness demanded satisfaction, and at the cross Christ provided it by dying. Therefore the cross was a manifestation of divine justice.

It was also history's greatest manifestation of love. Paul said that "God demonstrates his own love for us in this: While we were still sinners, Christ died for us" (Romans 5:8). John says in 1 John

4:10, "This is love: not that we loved God, but that he loved us and sent his Son as an atoning sacrifice for our sins."

On the cross Jesus was the representative man—the representative *condemned* man. God's wrath therefore burned against Him. So the cross was a divine action against the sinless Son of God on our behalf. The prophet Isaiah anticipated this crucial aspect of Christ's death some seven centuries earlier: "It was the Lord's will to crush him and cause him to suffer" (Isaiah 53:10).

Isaiah also knew that Christ's death would be vicarious; it would be for us. The prophet's language is deeply moving: "He was pierced for our transgressions, he was crushed for our iniquities; the punishment that brought us peace was upon him, and by his wounds we are healed. We all, like sheep, have gone astray, each of us has turned to his own way; and the Lord has laid on him the iniquity of us all" (Isaiah 53:5–6).

The vicariousness (the in-place-of-us) nature of Christ's death, and God's role in that death, fill the prophet's mind. Jesus was "stricken by God" (v. 4), but not for His own sins. Isaiah said, "The Lord has laid on him the iniquity of us all. . . . The Lord makes his life a guilt offering. . . . He bore the sin of many, and made intercession for the transgressors" (vv. 6, 10, 12).

These two ideas—God's role in Christ's death and the vicarious, substitutionary nature of that death—must be grasped if we are to have assurance of salvation. What they mean is that God Himself has provided for our salvation. And this is the ground of our assurance of salvation. If God is satisfied with Christ's death on the cross, what have we to fear?

From whence this fear and unbelief,
If God, our Father, put to grief
His spotless Son for me?
Can He, the righteous Judge of me,
Condemn me for that debt of sin
Which, Lord, was charged to Thee?
If Thou hast my discharge procured,
And freely in my place endured
The whole of wrath divine;
Payment God will not twice demand,
First at my bleeding Surety's hand,
And then again at mine.
Turn, then, my soul unto thy rest;
The merits of thy great High Priest
Speak peace and liberty;
Trust in His efficacious blood,
Nor fear thy banishment from God,
Since Jesus died for thee.

—AUGUSTUS MONTAGUE TOPLADY

The point is clear: adequate provision for salvation has been made. It satisfies God and, therefore, should satisfy us. That inner peace that we call assurance comes from knowing what God has done for us—and believing it. It comes from knowing and believing that the basis of salvation is what God has done for us by sending His Son to be the propitiation for our sins.

Two

The Way of
SALVATION
*What sinful people must do to be saved
and what God does to save them*

Sooner or later everyone who faces the fact of sin and the judgment to come inquires about the way of salvation. Of course, not every inquirer uses the expression "the way of salvation." That expression may be familiar only to people who read the Bible and are accustomed to thinking of life as a journey, with either heaven or hell as the final destination. A demon-possessed girl in ancient Philippi announced to the city that Paul and Silas were proclaiming "the way of salvation" (Acts 16:17 NASB).

When serious people think about heaven and hell, they ask simple questions about the way of salvation. The man in charge of the jail in Philippi, where Paul and Silas were kept, wanted to know about the way of salvation. He asked, "What must I do to be saved?" (Acts 16:30). His question was a natural one, because we feel almost instinctively that we must do *something*. What must we do? The answer to that question reveals the way of salvation.

Is there something we *can* do? All that we can do (and *must* do) is repent and believe the gospel. God is responsible to forgive us, redeem us, justify us, and reconcile us to Himself. What *we* do is simple; what *God* does is rich and complex. And as we shall see, God's part is the true source of peace and assurance.

WHAT WE MUST DO TO BE SAVED

In that Philippian jail, the jailer was terrified by an earthquake that sprang open the prison doors and snapped off the prisoners' chains. No doubt the jailer had heard Paul and Silas pray and sing praises to God. He may have sensed immediately that the earthquake was God's answer to their prayers. Fearing that all the prisoners had escaped, he was about to kill himself, but something stopped him: Paul's assurance that no one had escaped. Trembling on his knees, the jailer asked the apostles what he had to do to be saved. They told him to "believe in the Lord Jesus" (Acts 16:31). If he did, Paul said, he would be saved.

Saved from what? From the future wrath of God. In most—if not all—of his messages, Paul warned his listeners that judgment was coming (Acts 17:31; 20:26; 24:15, 24; 26:20). The gospel is the good news that sinners can avoid God's wrath. Paul defined his message as "the gospel of the grace of God" (Acts 20:24 NASB). Grace is God's kindness toward people, as demonstrated by His sending His Son to be the Savior of the world. God doesn't want to judge us; He wants to save us. That's the reason for the cross. But we must do our part. Our part is almost unbelievably simple. As Paul told the jailer, all we have to do to be saved is believe in the Lord Jesus.

Is that all—just believe? Yes. But there is more to the story than meets the eye. We take for granted that the account of the jailer's conversion is highly condensed. In Philippi, Paul said the same things he had said elsewhere—that Jesus was a Savior who had been crucified, laid in a tomb, and then raised from the dead. And many witnesses could testify to the truth of these things. Before his arrest, Paul would have told the people in Philippi that forgiveness of sins was granted to all who believed in Jesus (Acts 13:23–48).

The jailer had undoubtedly heard those things, either as a listener to Paul and Silas as they preached on the streets of Philippi or in the jail itself from someone else. Hence, when he heard Paul's answer to his anguished question, telling him to believe in the Lord Jesus, he knew that he had to believe certain things about Jesus—who He was and what He had done. He knew he had to believe that Jesus was more than a man and that God had raised Him from the dead (Romans 10:9). That, at the bare minimum, was what he believed.

Is that really all he had to do—just believe? Yes, if we take for granted that a fuller version of the story would have said that he was repentant. His subsequent actions show that he not only believed, he also repented.

Repentance

The word *repentance* isn't in the account of the jailer's conversion, but other passages in Acts indicate that Paul always urged his listeners to repent, as if belief were impossible without repentance.

For example, in Athens Paul concluded his message to the city's intellectuals with this call to repentance: "God is now declaring to men that *all* people everywhere should *repent*, because He has fixed a day in which He will judge the world in righteousness through a Man whom He has appointed, having furnished proof to all men by raising Him from the dead" (Acts 17:30–31 NASB, emphasis added).

Some of Paul's listeners believed him. They repented and believed. A few years later, when Paul reviewed his work in Asia Minor (modern Turkey) before a delegation of elders from Ephesus, he linked repentance with faith. Paul reminded them that he had preached publicly and from house to house, "solemnly testifying to both Jews and Greeks of repentance toward God and faith in our Lord Jesus Christ" (Acts 20:21 NASB).

That was what Paul told everyone everywhere—that they had to repent and believe in Jesus. On trial before King Agrippa, Paul told the king how he had become a Christian and what he had been doing since that time. He told the king that he had seen a blinding light from heaven and heard the voice from heaven of One who identified Himself as Jesus. He commissioned Paul to be a preacher. "So, King Agrippa," Paul said, "I did not prove disobedient to the heavenly vision, but kept declaring both to those of Damascus first, and also at Jerusalem and then throughout all the region of Judea, and even to the Gentiles, that they should *repent* and turn to God, performing deeds appropriate to repentance" (Acts 26:19–20 NASB, emphasis added). We'll look at what it means to repent.

Paul told everyone everywhere that they should repent and

turn to God because that is what he was told to preach. Of course, that isn't all he was told to preach; he was also told to preach that men and women everywhere should believe in Jesus. Those were his twin themes: repentance toward God and faith in the Lord Jesus Christ. These themes were basic to what Paul called "the gospel of the grace of God" (Acts 20:24 NASB). In sound preaching, neither can be omitted. Paul preached them, and we preach them. They are basic; they are the irreducible minimum content of biblical preaching.

The order in which Paul presented them was natural and consistent with their use in the New Testament: repentance followed by belief. The order is natural, because repentance is a change of mind, without which belief in Jesus would be impossible. A repentant person has a changed (i.e., different) attitude toward himself and his sin and toward God and judgment and Christ. Without the change indicated by the word *repentance*, no one would believe the gospel.

Some people visualize the call to repentance as depicting a comical figure with a long beard and raggedy robe, carrying a sandwich board that reads "Repent!"

John the Baptist came preaching repentance, but his call to repentance was a message of hope. "Repent," he said, "for the kingdom of heaven is at hand" (Matthew 3:2 NASB). Jesus began His work by preaching exactly the same message: "Repent, for the kingdom of heaven is at hand" (Matthew 4:17 NASB). The message could be paraphrased and expanded to say, "Repent, because God has something good to give you. Repent, the kingdom of heaven is open to as many as will accept it."

The command to repent is linked to two themes: the coming judgment and an infinitely better alternative—the kingdom of heaven. Seen in this light, repentance is a fitting part of "the gospel of the grace of God." God wants to save us, hence the command to repent and believe the good news. God asks no more, but He could not ask less. We must repent, and we must believe the gospel.

Repentance is a change of mind resulting in changed attitudes. It is *not* penance, which is an act of reparation or self-punishment. Penance could be said to be an attempt to atone for one's sin—which can't be done (Romans 3:20). Both John the Baptist and Paul asked for "fruit [or 'deed'] in keeping with repentance." What they wanted was not penance, but evidence that a person had repented and believed the gospel (Matthew 3:8 NASB; cf. Acts 26:20).

Belief

Many sincere Christians fret about belief; they worry that their faith is not strong enough. The Bible doesn't talk about faith that saves in terms of strength or weakness. It merely asks us to believe. Of course, there is a difference between belief that agrees that certain things about Jesus are true and belief that results in action, such as confessing that Jesus is Lord. The one is intellectual assent; the other is genuine faith. Consider the demons in Matthew 8:29–30 and James 2:19 who believed some correct doctrines about God and Christ, yet failed to trust God ultimately.

One of the apostle John's favorite words is the verb "to believe." (Curiously, perhaps, he does not use the noun form "belief.") John uses that verb ninety-nine times in his gospel. In his first epistle, he likens it to the ordinary belief we practice every day. John said, "We accept man's testimony, but God's testimony is greater because it is the testimony of God, which he has given about his Son" (1 John 5:9).

Therefore, believing is receiving the testimony that someone gives as true. It means to be persuaded of the truth of something. John reminded us that we receive the testimony people give, and he used this to illustrate belief in God. Under normal circumstances we believe each other. If I have a doctor's appointment, I keep it, believing that the doctor will see me. And if my furnace is on the fritz, the repairman fixes it, believing that I will pay him.

This is somewhat remarkable, because our testimony is not always entirely reliable. Why not? For at least three reasons. First, we can lie. Second, we can misinterpret what we hear or see, so that our version of a conversation or event is distorted. Third, we can forget the truth about something and, in attempting to remember, confuse fact with fancy. Nevertheless, we believe each other. Society could not function if we did not take what most people tell us at face value.

John's twofold point is that believing is essentially the same, whether we believe people or God, *and* that it should be easier to believe God than to believe each other. God cannot lie, does not misinterpret what He hears or sees, and never forgets anything. Accordingly, His testimony is 100 percent reliable. To say otherwise is to call God a liar (1 John 5:10).

Probably no one reading this considers God a liar. The problem many wrestle with is fear that ordinary belief is not enough. Yet John tells us that believing God is essentially the same as believing other people, only easier. It's easier because God is God, not a man. Belief (or faith) is valid or not valid according to its object. We may believe a lie strongly, or we may have complete faith in a scoundrel. But our faith is misplaced—and therefore useless.

Faith in God, on the other hand, is never misplaced. Faith in God is saving faith, not because one believes strongly, but because he believes in the Savior. When a person first believes in the Lord Jesus, he has done all he can do to be saved. But that is enough, for at that moment God Himself assumes complete responsibility for his salvation. Keeping us saved is God's responsibility. His honor is at stake. That is why we can rest in the assurance of salvation.

WHAT GOD DOES FOR OUR SALVATION

What happens when a person repents and believes in the Lord Jesus? He is saved. Paul said, "If you confess with your mouth Jesus as Lord, and believe in your heart that God raised Him from the dead, you will be saved" (Romans 10:9 NASB).

This raises questions about the part God plays in saving us. He saves us; but *how* exactly does He do it? Does He decide to overlook our sins in exchange for our willingness to believe in Him? Does He forgive us out of the kindness of His heart? Or does He remove our guilt and make us fit for His presence? Assuming for the moment that He does indeed remove our guilt and make us fit for His presence, is the arrangement permanent or conditional?

The right answers to these questions give us assurance of salvation. Wrong answers doom us to uncertainty and unhappiness.

The first thing to make clear in our minds is that salvation is entirely God's work. The Father sent the Son to be the Savior of the world; the Son provided a righteous basis for salvation; and the Holy Spirit makes the saving work effective in all who believe. We can't save ourselves. Except for the repenting and believing—which we must do—God does it all, as the following passage from Titus makes plain: "But when the kindness of God our Savior and His love for mankind appeared, He saved us, not on the basis of deeds which we have done in righteousness, but according to His mercy, by the washing of regeneration and renewing by the Holy Spirit, whom He poured out upon us richly through Jesus Christ our Savior" (Titus 3:4–6 NASB).

In that passage, God is called our Savior, Jesus Christ is called our Savior, and the Holy Spirit—although not called Savior—saves us by applying Christ's work on the cross to us individually. It's obvious why that paragraph is a favorite of many. Among other things, it underlines the point made earlier—that salvation is God's work, not ours. Except for repenting and believing—which contribute absolutely nothing toward the availability of salvation —we do nothing. God does it all. The most we can do is say yes to the Savior.

Many other texts tell us that when we respond to the good news God saves us. Among the best known is Ephesians 2:8–10: "For it is by grace that you have been saved, through faith—and this not from yourselves, it is the gift of God—not by works, so that no one can boast. For we are God's workmanship."

This raises a question that troubles some people: Could we have become Christians without supernatural help? Did we need help from the Holy Spirit of God to repent and believe? The question is interesting, but all we need to know is that God commands us to repent and believe the gospel. It doesn't matter where the desire to obey comes from, or at what point in the process the Holy Spirit gives whatever help may be necessary. All that matters is that, having heard the Word, we respond in faith.

Then God takes over. God assumes complete responsibility for our eternal security. He Himself guarantees the permanence of our salvation. That is clear from various texts, including Ephesians 1:13–14, which lays out the steps to salvation—from hearing the good news to the conclusion of the matter in heaven: "You also were included in Christ when you heard the word of truth, the gospel of your salvation. Having believed, you were marked in him with a seal, the promised Holy Spirit, who is a deposit guaranteeing our inheritance until the redemption of those who are God's possession—to the praise of his glory."

That remarkable passage assures us that our job is to hear the Word of God and believe it. Having done that, we have done all we can do. At that point, God takes over; He gives us the gift of the Holy Spirit—who is the guarantee of our salvation. But is He a *permanent* gift? That's the question that troubles believers who fear that they may lose their salvation. They worry that if they commit a horrible sin, the Holy Spirit will leave them. David expresses that fear in Psalm 51:11. Therefore the question is, Is the Holy Spirit a *permanent* gift?

The answer is yes. The Holy Spirit comes into our lives to stay. This is clearly indicated by the terms "seal" and "deposit" used in the passage. An ordinary dictionary defines a seal as "something that confirms, ratifies, or makes secure [or] that authenticates." The Holy Spirit is God's stamp of ownership on us. We belong to God. If divine ownership were not permanent, God would not have used the word *seal*.

The Holy Spirit's presence in us is also like earnest money, or a down payment. He is the present pledge of divine seriousness about salvation. God means business; He will make good on His promise of eternal life, and the presence of the Holy Spirit guarantees it.

Another angle that should be considered is the irreversibility of what the Holy Spirit does in us. Think for a moment about that text in Titus that tells us we have been given "the washing of rebirth and renewal by the Holy Spirit, whom [God] poured out on us generously" (3:4–6). Rebirth (or new birth) and renewal (or new life) are not reversible conditions. Can anybody be born again and then become "unborn"?

Suppose it were possible to lose the Holy Spirit. If it were, we'd revert to being "dead in [our] transgressions and sins" (Ephesians 2:1, cf. v. 5). Not only that, we would also be "separate from Christ," with all that entails (Ephesians 2:12). Among other things, it would mean that we were ordered out of "the kingdom of the Son

[God] loves" and returned to "the dominion of darkness," from which He first rescued us (Colossians 1:13).

The point is clear: when we first believe the gospel, what God does for us cannot be changed. We can't go back to square one— that place where we were unpardoned, unredeemed, and unreconciled to God—in short, the place where we were without God in the world, and therefore unsaved.

What *does* God do for us when we believe the good news? What does He do in addition to giving us the Holy Spirit? He does many things, but we shall think about only four or five divine activities done on our behalf: God forgives us, redeems us, justifies us, and reconciles us to Himself. Furthermore, He adopts us. Whether we consider each of these benefits separately or in combination, their irreversibility gives us a solid basis for assurance.

God Forgives Us

No lovelier concept exists in Scripture than forgiveness, perhaps because we sense instinctively that we don't deserve it and that it doesn't come cheap. At the Last Supper Jesus took the cup and "gave thanks and offered it to them, saying, 'Drink from it, all of you. This is my blood of the covenant, which is poured out for many for *the forgiveness* of sins'" (Matthew 26:27–28, emphasis added).

The costliness of forgiveness is clear from the New Testament link between forgiveness and Christ's death. For example, after accusing the high priest and his associates of direct responsibility for the death of Jesus, Peter went on to say that "God exalted him to his own right hand as Prince and Savior that he might give repentance and *forgiveness of sins* to Israel" (Acts 5:31, emphasis added).

In nearly every New Testament reference to forgiveness, Christ's death is the basis of it. As Paul said, "In him we have redemption through his blood, the forgiveness of sins" (Ephesians 1:7). The text makes at least two points. First, forgiveness doesn't come cheap. It's available only "through his blood," which is Paul's way of saying that Christ had to die before God could offer forgiveness. Second, forgiveness is closely linked to redemption—about which more will be said later.

We can't have a clear idea of the costliness of forgiveness unless we know what forgiveness is. Pardon and forgiveness are practically the same, so that to be forgiven is to be pardoned. What do the words mean? An African equivalent (*oku etchela*) explains the concept nicely. The African word means literally "to give up something or somebody." To forgive is to give up a just claim against somebody—and in giving it up to suffer loss of some kind. To forgive is to give up the right to collect something that is owed. As W. H. Griffith Thomas explains,

> The one who pardons really accepts the results of the wrong done to him in order that he may exempt the other from any punishment. Thus . . . when a man cancels a debt, he of necessity loses the amount, and if he pardons an insult or a blow, he accepts in his person the injury done in either case. So human pardon may be said to cancel at its own expense any wrong

done, and this principle of the innocent suffering for the guilty is the fundamental truth of the Atonement.[1]

Clearly, even genuine human forgiveness doesn't come cheap. The person who forgives accepts loss or injury of some kind and gives up a claim to compensation. In this sense, human forgiveness is like divine forgiveness. As Thomas goes on to observe,

> Human forgiveness . . . really illuminates, vindicates and necessitates the Divine pardon, for forgiveness is mercy which has first satisfied the principle of justice. On this ground we hold that Christ's death made it possible for God to forgive sin. What His justice demanded His love provided. This fact of the death of Jesus Christ as the foundation of pardon is unchallengeable in the New Testament.[2]

Divine pardon does not come cheap. In order that God may give up His claim against sinners, at least two things are required: the sinner must face his judge, and a suitable substitute must be found for the sinner. That is what happened at the cross. Christ offered Himself to God as the sinner's substitute and represented him before God. At the cross, God's wrath against sin became directed against Christ. Christ's death satisfied divine claims against sin. In this way, Jesus Christ's death on the cross is the basis of divine forgiveness. As Paul says in Ephesians 1:7, we have forgiveness "through his blood."

We see the beauty of divine forgiveness. It's not like human forgiveness that overlooks an injury and sometimes brings it up again. God doesn't sweep our sins under the rug. If He did, we'd worry that He might become tired of our fresh sins and failures and take back His forgiveness. But He doesn't do that, because divine forgiveness is based on justice. God can release us completely; He can give up His claims against us as sinners, because Christ paid what we owed.

We sometimes sing the refrain,

> *Jesus paid it all*
> *All to Him I owe;*
> *Sin had left a crimson stain,*
> *He washed it white as snow.*
>
> —ELVINA M. HALL

Those words are comforting. Micah said in prayer, "Who is a God like You, who pardons iniquity and passes over the rebellious act of the remnant of His possession? He does not retain His anger forever, because He delights in unchanging love" (Micah 7:18 NASB).

The apostle John undoubtedly knew that text in Micah and loved it. But every time John quoted it, he most likely added that God pardons not only because He delights in unchanging love and, therefore, *likes* to forgive His people, but also because He is "faithful and just" (1 John 1:9). In forgiving us, God is just, because Christ's death enabled Him to forgive us without compromising His holy character. God is always faithful; it's His nature to be faithful. But what does faithfulness have to do with forgiveness?

The answer is simple and profound: God is faithful to His promise to forgive. Furthermore, He may be said to be faithful to Christ, who intercedes on behalf of His people. By forgiving us when we sin, God honors the One who died and now lives to make intercession for us.

It's reassuring to know that when God forgives us He does so in complete consistency with His character. Forgiveness is not given grudgingly. God gives it freely and never withdraws it. How can He? Paul asked, "Who is he that condemns?" Then he answered his own question: "Christ Jesus, who died—more than that, who was raised to life—is at the right hand of God and is also interceding for us" (Romans 8:34).

If Christ who died for us does not condemn us, who can? The answer is obvious: no one. But the fact that no one can condemn us is not Paul's primary point. His point is that Christ does not condemn us; instead, He intercedes for us. Since this is true, why should we fret about the possibility of losing salvation? We can't lose it. The risen Christ is at the right hand of God, representing us. His presence in heaven assures us that everything is in order. As Paul said, "He . . . was delivered over because of our transgressions, and was raised because of our justification" (Romans 4:25 NASB). We'll be looking at the meanings of *justification* and *being justified* next.

The phrase "he . . . was delivered over" refers to Christ's death. He was put to death because of our transgressions. And because His death was adequate grounds for our justification, we can have assurance of salvation. Because He was raised, we know

we are justified. So Christ's resurrection is proof that we have
been justified. And as we shall see, justification is as irreversible
as forgiveness.

God Justifies Us

We need more than forgiveness. Forgiveness is not enough.
It's not enough because it doesn't undo completely the damage sin
does. Theologians note three results of sin in the garden of Eden:
guilt, condemnation, and alienation (separation) from God. What
we need is cancellation of *all* the results of sin: the removal of
guilt, the lifting of condemnation, and an end to separation from
God. In short, what we need is justification, which deals completely with all the consequences of sin.

Justification is a familiar New Testament word. It was one of
Paul's favorites, as is clear from the following texts:

> *For all have sinned and fall short of the glory of God, and* are justified
> *freely by his grace through the redemption that came by Christ Jesus.*
> (Romans 3:23–24, emphasis added)

> *He was delivered over to death for our sins and was raised to life for our*
> justification. (Romans 4:25, emphasis added)

> *Therefore, since we have been* justified *through faith, we have peace*
> *with God through our Lord Jesus Christ.* (Romans 5:1, emphasis
> added)

We need a simple definition of justification. W. H. Griffith Thomas presents a good one: "Justification is that act of God whereby He accepts and accounts us righteous, though in ourselves unrighteous."[3] That definition makes the supremely important point that justification is an act of God; it is something that He does for us. God justifies us freely without our having earned the favor. Justification is entirely His work on our behalf. Christians who remember this great truth *know* they are permanently saved.

Our definition of justification also points to two benefits that come to those whom God justifies: imputed righteousness first and then acceptance, in that order.

Though seldom necessary for ordinary conversation, "impute" and "imputed" are words that we should understand. They appear in a few translations of the English Bible in passages such as Psalm 32:2: "Blessed is the man to whom the Lord does not *impute* iniquity, and in whose spirit there is no deceit" (NKJV, emphasis added).

Paul uses the word in one of his neat summaries of the gospel: "God was in Christ, reconciling the world unto himself, not *imputing* their trespasses unto them; and hath committed unto us the word of reconciliation" (2 Corinthians 5:19 KJV, emphasis added).

The word appears in other important texts, but most modern translations of the Greek text use "reckon," "count," or "accredit." All of these words—including "impute"—accurately convey the idea intended by the Greek word that Paul used. Quite simply, God credits us with righteousness that we do not inherently possess. It becomes ours when we believe God. As Paul said,

"Abraham believed God, and it was credited to him as righteousness. Now when a man works, his wages are not credited to him as a gift, but as an obligation. However, to the man who does not work but trusts God who justifies the wicked, his faith is credited as righteousness" (Romans 4:3–5).

Our definition echoes that passage. "Justification is an act of God whereby He . . . accounts us righteous, though in ourselves unrighteous." Justification does not change us in the sense that we cease to be essentially sinful and become intrinsically sinless and righteous. We are still sinners, but God regards us as righteous.

To understand this, we can think about Christ on the cross. When He was crucified, He assumed responsibility for our sins, and God treated Him as if He were sin itself. Yet in Himself, He did not change; He did not become evil. If He had become personally evil, He would have been disqualified as our substitute. So He remained personally holy, yet *credited* with all our sins. In the same way, God now treats us as if we were righteous. He *credits* us with righteousness by virtue of our relationship with Christ.

It's terribly important to remember that justification is not a state of righteousness. A justified person is essentially no more righteous than before conversion. But he is *declared* to be righteous. And since God declares it, the declaration is all that is needed. Justification is an act of God whereby He clears us of all charges against us, imputes righteousness to us, and accepts us.

We begin to see the rich meaning of justification. It's richer than our definition and includes at least four (not two) actions on God's part: He forgives us, He clears us of all charges against us,

He imputes (reckons or credits) righteousness to us, and He accepts us. These things happen simultaneously, but we think about them in sequence to understand them more easily. The heart of justification is the middle two actions: God clears us of all charges against us, and He credits us with righteousness.

Knowing that God clears us of all charges—and how—gives us the assurance that the matter is settled forever. We are eternally safe. Everyone knows what is meant when one is cleared of charges. In an American court, an accused man is considered innocent until proven guilty. Nevertheless, he may be facing serious charges. He is accused of crime. If the jury finds him innocent, he is cleared of charges and leaves the courtroom a free man. The jury's decision exonerates him.

Early in the twentieth century, Captain Alfred Dreyfus was framed by fellow officers in the French army and sent to Devil's Island. Under pressure from people such as Emile Zola, the French government pardoned Dreyfus. To the government's amazement, Captain Dreyfus was outraged by the pardon and refused it. He demanded exoneration, which he eventually received. To have accepted a pardon would have been to admit guilt. Only guilty men need to be pardoned. Dreyfus wanted to be declared innocent and cleared of all charges.

In God's court no one is exonerated and pronounced innocent of all charges. Just the opposite. Paul goes to great effort in Romans to show that "all have sinned and fall short of the glory of God" (Romans 3:23).

When we say that a justified person is cleared of charges, we

don't mean that God or a jury in heaven finds that person innocent. What we mean is that God finds us guilty. He pronounces
sentence of death, and He executes us! And *then* He clears us of
charges. That may sound a bit confusing since we are still living.
And yet He has indeed executed us—in the person of His Son.
The merits of Christ's death are transferred to our account, so to
speak. God now views us as if we had been duly punished for our
sins. Therefore He clears us of charges.

The idea is illustrated by the state's treatment of a convicted
felon at the completion of his sentence. The state cannot keep him
in prison one day longer. Having served his sentence, he is cleared
of charges. That is our situation. In God's eyes our sentence has
been served. We know, of course, that Christ suffered, not us. But
since God reckons the full value of that death to our account, He
clears us of charges.

God Accepts Us

When we are justified, we are accepted by God. He accepts us
willingly and gladly, not grudgingly, as if His love overcame His
holiness but left Him uneasy. He accepts us because He Himself
has made us acceptable in His sight. We express this great truth in
a lovely hymn:

> *"In the Beloved" accepted am I,*
> *Risen, ascended, and seated on high;*
> *Saved from all sin thro' His infinite grace,*
> *With the redeemed ones accorded a place.*

> *"In the Beloved" I went to the tree,*
> *There, in His Person, by faith I may see*
> *Infinite wrath rolling over His head,*
> *Infinite grace, for He died in my stead.*[4]
>
> —CIVILLA D. MARTIN

The Beloved is our Lord Jesus Christ. The hymn echoes the Bible, where we read that God has made us "accepted in the beloved. In whom we have redemption through his blood, the forgiveness of sins, according to the riches of his grace" (Ephesians 1:6–7 KJV).

The last lines of the hymn's chorus make the ground of acceptance clear: "God sees my Savior and then He sees me 'In the Beloved,' accepted and free."

God has made us acceptable to Himself by crediting us with righteousness. And that great truth—as we have seen—is at the heart of justification. Great assurance exists in knowing that forgiveness and acceptance are righteous acts of God. He forgives us because no outstanding charges are brought against us. He accepts us because He Himself has made us fit for His presence.

Fit for His presence. Accepted. Not because of any merits in ourselves either before or after conversion but because God has justified us. As Paul explained,

> *Everyone has sinned and is far away from God's saving presence. But by the free gift of God's grace all are put right with him through Christ Jesus, who sets them free. God offered him, so that by his blood he should*

*become the means by which people's sins are forgiven through their faith
in him. God did this in order to demonstrate that he is righteous. . . . In
this way God shows that he himself is righteous and that he puts right
everyone who believes in Jesus.* (Romans 3:23–26 TEV)

God "puts us right." That's what justification really is: God's
work of putting us right with Him. And the beauty of it is its permanence. As W. H. Griffith Thomas explains,

Justification is complete and never repeated. It relates to our
spiritual position in the sight of God and covers the whole of
our life past, present, and future. Forgiveness is only nega-
tive, the removal of condemnation. Justification is also positive, the removal of guilt and the bestowal of a perfect standing before God. In a word, justification means reinstatement.[5]

That's what it means: *reinstatement*. In this way, God has
taken care of all the results of sin: guilt is removed, condemnation
is lifted, and spiritual separation is ended. A justified person has
been forgiven, all charges against him have been removed, and he
has been reinstated.

That is precisely what Paul had in mind when he posed the
questions in Romans 8:33–35. "Who will bring any charge against
those whom God has chosen?" The answer is no one, because
guilt has been removed. "Who is he that condemns?" Again, the
answer is no one. Condemnation has been lifted. "Who shall separate us from the love of Christ?" No one! Separation has ended;

reconciliation has been achieved so that nothing in all creation will ever be able to separate us from the love of God that is in Christ Jesus our Lord.

No believer should worry about eternal security. Heaven is as certain for all who believe in Jesus as the Word of God is true.

God Redeems Us

The words *redeem* and *redemption* in the Bible are like the word *propitiation*—largely forgotten. Of course, the words are used in grocery stores that accept coupons in exchange for merchandise. In places of business this word has been redefined. Christians ought to take the trouble to learn how it is used in the Bible. As we said before, assurance of salvation depends on knowledge. Only to the extent that we understand what the Bible teaches about salvation can we know for certain that we are eternally safe. Redemption is an important aspect of salvation. It follows that we ought to understand it.

To redeem (in one biblical sense) is to free from captivity by payment of a ransom. The word evokes images of slaves or prisoners and negotiations to buy or free them. In ancient times (long before Jesus came to earth), slavery was an accepted institution. Because it existed, the Bible described it. Old Testament law dealt with the institution of slavery and made provision for freeing slaves. That must be what Jesus had in mind when He spoke of His impending death as a "ransom." Mark 10:45 says, "For even the Son of Man did not come to be served, but to serve, and to give his life as a ransom for many."

His death ("giving His life") would be a ransom. Later, Paul said that "Christ Jesus . . . gave himself as a ransom for all men" (1 Timothy 2:5–6). The concept is strange to us, although certainly it was not to people who lived in ancient times. Naturally, we ask why Christ should have had to pay a ransom. Were we slaves? If so, who enslaved us, and to whom would Jesus pay a ransom? And how would He pay it?

The Bible doesn't answer all those questions. It doesn't say to whom Jesus paid a ransom. However, it does say that we were slaves—slaves to sin—and it says that nothing less than Christ's blood would suffice to buy us out of that moral bondage. Paul spoke of himself (perhaps before his conversion) as "sold as a slave to sin" (Romans 7:14). Sin had taken him prisoner.

Redemption (that is, rescue or deliverance) was possible only through Christ's death. Thinking about the moral trap he was in, Paul cried out, "What a wretched man I am! Who will rescue me from this body of death?" (Romans 7:24). Paul immediately answered his own question: "Thanks be to God—through Jesus Christ our Lord!" (v. 25). Nothing less than Christ's death was acceptable as a ransom price. By dying, Christ paid the required ransom.

An English missionary once stood watching a long line of Angolan slaves shuffle by on their way to the coast, where they would be sold to cocoa bean plantation owners. They were tied to each other by a rope around the waist. Eventually the Englishman stopped the line of moving figures. He called to the slave master and asked for the release of a boy and his sister. They were about twelve years old and had been kidnapped in the Songo country.

The slave master demanded a heavy price—so many gun barrels, so many kegs of powder, so many bolts of cloth, and so on. The missionary paid the price, and the boy and his sister were cut out of the line. The loose ends of the rope were tied together, and the line started moving again, leaving the boy and his sister behind.

The children were terrified. They had never seen white men before. But the Englishman spoke kindly to them, telling them he had ransomed them. They were free to return to their own country and could leave as soon as he could find a guide for them.

The children understood his words but not his meaning. They never returned to the Songo country. Years later the missionary understood their refusal to leave. In their minds, they were now *his* slaves. The reason for their confusion was rooted in African tradition. According to their custom, only a relative could free a slave. That kindhearted Englishman was not a relative. Although he believed he had freed them, the children believed he had bought them.

That true story brings to mind Old Testament references to a kinsman-redeemer. A kinsman is a blood relative. Speaking of Christ, the Bible says that "since the children have flesh and blood, he too shared in their humanity so that by his death he might destroy him who holds the power of death—that is, the devil—and free those who all their lives were held in slavery by their fear of death" (Hebrews 2:14–15).

In Christ, God became man in order to be able to die, and by dying, free (redeem) us from slavery to sin and death. But that is not the main point the writers of the New Testament want to make in their references to redemption. Their point is twofold. First, having been "bought," we now belong to God. Second, redemption's price is a great incentive to holy living. For example, in Titus Paul says that our Savior Jesus Christ "gave himself for us to redeem us from all wickedness and to purify for himself a people that are his very own, eager to do what is good" (Titus 2:14).

It's a brief statement, but it makes a point: Christ Himself was the price given for us, so we now belong to Him and, as His people, ought to be "eager to do what is good." Peter said much the same thing. He reminded his readers that they had been redeemed from "the empty way of life" handed down to them from their forefathers, "not with perishable things such as silver or gold . . . but with the precious blood of Christ, a lamb without blemish or defect" (1 Peter 1:18–19).

In each passage, it is clear that the price of redemption was Christ's blood. Two other facts are also clear: first, redemption frees us to be the people of God. We are "his very own" (Titus 2:14). Second, redemption is *an accomplished fact*. On that basis the apostles exhort their respective audiences to shape up as Christians. Substandard living is inconsistent with at least three realities: (1) the fact that Jesus is our Savior, (2) the terrible price He had to pay to save us, and (3) the claim God has on us as "a people that are his very own."

Neither Paul nor Peter suggests that redemption is conditional or that redeemed people can become unredeemed if they fail in some way. Redemption is an accomplished, irreversible fact. It is as certain as forgiveness, because it is tied to the same thing:

Christ's death on our behalf. He who gave Himself for us as a ransom died for us as a propitiation. And in saving us, God saves us *for Himself.* He wants us to be "a people that are his very own," whom He will never reject. As Paul says in Romans 11:29, God's gifts and His call "are irrevocable." Redemption is forever.

What that means, of course, is that if we have been redeemed, we cannot become unredeemed; we cannot lose our salvation.

God Reconciles Us

The dictionary defines the verb "to reconcile" as "to cause to be friendly again; to bring back to harmony." That is essentially how Scripture uses the term, although the concept is richer in Scripture. In the Bible reconciliation is less concerned with feelings than with relationships. Paul referred to reconciliation in his writings: "If, when we were God's enemies, we were reconciled to him through the death of his Son, how much more, having been reconciled, shall we be saved through his life!" (Romans 5:10).

The expression "God's enemies" describes a relationship, not necessarily an attitude. Reconciliation assumes a previous relationship of hostility or enmity. Friends don't need to be reconciled to each other. Were we God's enemies? The Bible says plainly that before conversion we were indeed His enemies. We may not have been personally conscious of antagonism toward God. As Paul explained, however, "The sinful mind is hostile to God. It does not submit to God's law, neither can it do so. Those controlled by the sinful nature cannot please God" (Romans 8:7–8).

The apostle James said virtually the same thing. As he explained, a sinful mind loves what God hates. James said, "Friendship with the world is hostility toward God. Therefore whoever wishes to be a friend of the world makes himself an enemy of God" (James 4:4 NASB).

It follows that salvation must include reconciliation with the benefits already considered in this booklet: forgiveness, justification, and redemption. Although we think about these benefits one at a time, they are just different aspects of the same salvation. Quite a few words are required to explain all that God does for us when He saves us. He meets *all* our spiritual needs. We need forgiveness, and He forgives us. We need justification, and He justifies us. We need redemption, and He redeems us. Reconciliation is His remedy for the state of enmity that prevailed between Him and us.

Reconciliation is *His* remedy; it is *His* work on our behalf. What is true of forgiveness, justification, and redemption is also true of reconciliation: it is a work of God; it is something He does for us. Paul explained, "Therefore, if anyone is in Christ, he is a new creation; the old has gone, the new has come! All this is from God, who reconciled us to himself through Christ and gave us the ministry of reconciliation: that God was reconciling the world to himself in Christ, not counting men's sins against them" (2 Corinthians 5:17–19).

Does that mean that we contribute nothing to reconciliation? Yes and no. Yes in the sense that we are powerless on our own to deal with any of sin's effects, including separation from God. If God had not wanted an end to the alienation between Himself and us, reconciliation would have been impossible. The initiative had to come from Him, and He alone was able to do something about the obstacles to reconciliation. He alone was (and is) able to accomplish reconciliation.

But we also have a part in reconciliation. That is clear from the rest of the text quoted above: "He has committed to us the message of reconciliation. We are therefore God's ambassadors, as though God were making his appeal through us. We implore you on Christ's behalf: Be reconciled to God" (2 Corinthians 5:19–20).

The phrase "be reconciled to God" calls for response to God's work. How can we respond? By obedience to the gospel. No other way exists; we are required to repent and believe. When we believe, we immediately receive all the benefits of salvation, including reconciliation with God.

Reconciliation is important, but it is merely one aspect of the same salvation that includes forgiveness, justification, redemption, and a few other rich benefits. As used in Romans 5:10, reconciliation is almost another way of saying justification. That becomes clear from a close reading of Romans 5:9–11:

> *Since we have now been* justified by his blood, *how much more shall we be saved from God's wrath through him! For if, when we were God's enemies, we were* reconciled to him through the death of his Son, *how much more, having been reconciled, shall we be saved through his life! Not only is this so, but we also rejoice in God through our Lord Jesus Christ, through whom we have now received reconciliation.* (emphasis added)

Justification and reconciliation are not exactly identical, but they are similar. A justified person has been cleared of charges and made right with God. Being made right with God, Paul wanted us to know, includes an end to that former alienation. Reconciliation has been accomplished.

Reconciliation creates a new relationship. That is what Paul intends to say in 2 Corinthians 5:17–18. A reconciled person is "in Christ"; he is a "new creation." And Paul added, "All this is from God, who reconciled us to himself through Christ."

All this should be reassuring to us as believers. Although we were formerly estranged from God and hostile to Him—though not necessarily *conscious* of hostility—we were reconciled to Him through the death of His Son. Reconciliation is a new standing with God, and because it is "from God," it is as permanent as justification. It rests upon the same foundation as forgiveness and justification and redemption—the death of Christ. Therefore, it is permanent. Having brought us back to Himself, God is not going to banish us again.

In a speech before the king of Israel, a woman of Tekoa said, "But God does not take away life; instead, he devises ways so that a banished person may not remain estranged from him" (2 Samuel 14:14).

The cross was God's way of ending our estrangement from Him. Only those who don't understand the implications of reconciliation are afraid that they may lose their salvation. If God reconciled them to Himself when they were enemies, is He likely to cast them out after they have become friends? No. Eighteenth-century hymn writer Catesby Paget expresses the peace of mind enjoyed by those who know they have been reconciled to God and who rest in that fact:

> *A mind at "perfect peace" with God;*
> *Oh, what a word is this!*
> *A sinner reconciled through blood;*
> *This, this indeed is peace*
> *By nature and by practice far—*
> *How very far from God!*
> *Yet now by grace brought nigh to Him,*
> *Through faith in Jesus' blood.*
> *So near, so very dear to God, I cannot nearer be;*
> *For in the person of His Son I am as near as He.*

God Adopts Us

Closely related to reconciliation is adoption, which means "the placing of a son." Although only Paul used the word in his epistles, other New Testament writers were aware of its implications. Paul says in Galatians 4:4–7,

> *But when the fullness of the time came, God sent forth His Son, born of a woman, born under the Law, so that He might redeem those who were under the Law, that we might receive the adoption as sons. Because you are sons, God has sent forth the Spirit of His Son into our hearts, crying, "Abba! Father!" Therefore you are no longer a slave, but a son; and if a son, then an heir through God.* (NASB)

Paul's first-century readers understood precisely what he was saying. They were familiar with the Roman custom of taking an outsider (not a member of the family) and making him a legal son and heir. As a consequence of the adoption ceremony, the new son did two things: he severed all ties with the past, and he took the new family name with all the privileges and responsibilities of legitimate sonship.

That double action—the cutting off of the past and the taking of a new identity and a new allegiance—is what Paul has in mind when he says in Romans 8:12–16,

> *Brothers, we have an obligation—but it is not to the sinful nature, to live according to it. For if you live according to the sinful nature, you will die; but if by the Spirit you put to death the misdeeds of the body, you will live, because those who are led by the Spirit of God are sons of God. For you did not receive a spirit that makes you a slave again to fear, but you received the Spirit of* [adoption unto] *sonship. And by him we cry, "Abba, Father." The Spirit himself testifies with our spirit that we are God's children.*

We see that reconciliation is not an end in itself. It is reconciliation *unto* something wonderful: the placing of us as children in God's family. Reconciliation and adoption are like two sides of the same coin. Reconciliation is concerned with an end to our alienation from God and the beginning of a new relationship. Adoption defines the new relationship with God. It is a relationship so strong that nothing less than adoption would suffice to illustrate it.

The two ideas are partly illustrated by the story of the Prodigal Son, the wayward young man who, when he was broke and hungry, decided to go home. Not knowing that his father was waiting for him, the guilt-ridden young man decided to ask his father to make him like one of the hired men. He believed that he was unworthy to be called a son. But his father brushed his request aside, sent for the best robe in the house, a ring for his finger, and sandals for his feet. "This son of mine . . . has been found," he said (Luke 15:24 NASB).

The father's running to meet the approaching Prodigal Son is a wonderful illustration of reconciliation and adoption. But the story only *partly* illustrates adoption. It's imperfect because the young wastrel really *was* his son. He was a genuine member of the family. The father reaffirmed his status as a true son. Adoption, on the other hand, deals with people who are not members of the family. Before God brings us home, we are, in Paul's words, "separate from Christ . . . having no hope and without God in the world" (Ephesians 2:12 NASB). We are enemies of God, needing reconciliation with God. But having been reconciled to God through the death of His Son, we are adopted. Hence, we "are no longer strangers and aliens, but . . . fellow citizens with the saints, and . . . of God's household" (Ephesians 2:19 NASB).

By an act of God that Paul called "the placing of a son" (the meaning of the Greek word Paul used), believers in Jesus have been designated sons of God. We are no longer outsiders; we are part of the family of God—which was God's intention all along. In Galatians 4:5 Paul says that God sent forth His Son in order to redeem us *and* give us "the adoption as sons" (NASB). Redemption would be incomplete without adoption. In another text, Paul emphasizes the truth that adoption was *always* God's intention for us. Paul said, "Before the foundation of the world . . . He predestined us to adoption as sons through Jesus Christ to Himself, according to the kind intention of His will" (Ephesians 1:4–5 NASB).

If we understand its implications, no other aspect of salvation appeals to our hearts as powerfully as adoption. God not only saves us from the penalty of sin, He makes us members of His household. What greater act of love could exist? The apostle John was amazed at such love. He said, "How great is the love the Father has lavished on us, that we should be called children of God! And that is what we are!" (1 John 3:1).

Think of sonship with reference to assurance of salvation. If a person could be saved and then lost, God would not only have to declare the offending person unforgiven, unjustified, unredeemed, and unreconciled, He would also have to tear up the adoption papers. He would have to say that the offender is no longer a child of God, no longer a member of the household of God. And that would also mean that God had recalled the Holy Spirit. According to Galatians 4:6, the Holy Spirit's presence in our lives is closely linked to adoption. "Because you are sons, God has sent forth the Spirit of His Son into our hearts, crying, 'Abba! Father!'" (NASB).

Is it likely that all that can be undone? Those who say yes have to answer several related questions. First, what *specific* sin is sufficient to cause God to sever relations with one of His children?

Second, if all that God does for us when we first believed can be undone, can it be done all over again? In other words, having been saved and then lost again, can we be saved again? If so, how many times? If we can be saved, then lost and saved again—presumably upon confession and belief—what happens if we die in the split second between lostness and renewal of salvation? Those are serious questions, and we will consider them later.

Meanwhile, it's important to remember that the benefits of salvation aren't given one at a time. To understand the many benefits of salvation, though, we must analyze them one at a time. This may give the impression that God forgives us first, *then* justifies us, and so on until He finishes the job. The truth is contrary. Except for things that necessarily remain undone (e.g., the resurrection of the body), full salvation is ours the instant we trust Christ as Savior. In the *same instant* we are: forgiven, justified, reconciled, regenerated, adopted, and so on.

Salvation is God's doing from start to finish. Is it reasonable to believe that God will undo all that He has done for us? No. We were sinners when He first saved us. He will not reject us if we fall short of perfection as believers.

All that God does for us is done with a view to the future. When the apostle John considered our relationship with the Lord as sons, his mind turned toward heaven. John said, "Dear friends, now we are children of God, and what we will be has not yet been made known. But we know that when he appears, we shall be like him, for we shall see him as he is" (1 John 3:2).

What we are *now*—children of God—determines what we

will be when He appears. Then, no one will mistake whose we are. We shall be like Him. We are His now, and we shall be His forever. As we sometimes sing,

The work which His goodness began,
The arm of His strength will complete;
His promise is Yea and Amen,
And never was forfeited yet.
Things future, nor things that are now,
Not all things below or above,
Can make Him His purpose forego,
Or sever my soul from His love.
My name from the palms of His hands
Eternity will not erase;
Imprest on His heart, it remains
In marks of indelible grace.
Yes! I to the end shall endure,
As sure as the earnest is given;
More happy, but not more secure,
The souls of the blessed in heaven.

—A. M. TOPLADY

Notes

1. W. H. Griffith Thomas, *The Principles of Theology* (London: Longman's, 1930), 58.

2. Ibid.

3. Ibid., 186.

4. *Accepted in the Beloved*. © Copyright 1930, renewed 1958, Hope Publishing Co. Used by permission.

5. Thomas, *Principles of Theology*, 186.

Three

The Question of SIN
Why saved people still sin

The first thing to understand is the fact that we sin. No such thing as a sinless Christian exists. True, a few Scripture texts *seem* to say that we don't sin. The universal experience of Christians, however, is that they do indeed sin, which suggests these verses that seem to say otherwise are subtler than they first appear. The texts in question do not teach sinlessness this side of the grave. Besides, much of the New Testament obviously assumes that Christians are both capable of sinning and at times guilty of it. For example, in dealing with elders who have been accused of wrongdoing, Paul said, "Do not entertain an accusation against an elder unless it is brought by two or three witnesses. *Those who sin* are to be rebuked publicly, so that the others may take warning" (1 Timothy 5:19–20, emphasis added).

That text alone makes the point, but for good measure we refer to James's statement that "we all stumble in many ways" (James 3:2). The apostles take for granted that we are sinful.

Hence the many warnings to abstain from sin, and the texts that tell the church how to deal with believers whose sins are public knowledge.

Why do Christians sin? Do they lose their salvation when they sin? These are serious questions, and they trouble many believers. Wrong answers deprive us of assurance that we belong to Christ. First, we sin because we are still sinful, even though we are saved. Second, when we sin, we do not lose our salvation; we do not become unsaved.

If we believed that genuine Christians *never* sinned, most of us would conclude that we personally had never been saved. On the other hand, if we believed that Christians could sin but lost their salvation the moment they sinned, we'd despair of ever knowing for certain that we were saved. The chronic uncertainty would drive us crazy if we permitted ourselves to think about it. Or, we'd give up, as many have done already.

On a visit home to his native Scotland, Fred Stanley Arnot, a pioneer missionary to Africa, was asked to write his favorite verse in a friend's Bible. Arnot wrote Psalm 23:3, and his friend was surprised by the saintly missionary's choice of texts. If Arnot had written Psalm 23:1, the friend would not have been surprised, because that verse is a great affirmation of faith: "The Lord is my shepherd; I shall not want" (KJV). Verse 3, on the other hand, is less an affirmation of faith than a statement of need or a confession of sin: "He restoreth my soul." Why did the missionary say that verse 3 was his favorite?

His journals explain. Fred Stanley Arnot had lived long

enough in trying circumstances to experience the deep need felt by all mature believers for forgiveness—not forgiveness of sins committed *before* conversion, but forgiveness of sins committed *after* conversion. The sins that troubled Fred Stanley Arnot's conscience were not fleshly; they were spiritual. His sins may have included anger at God's apparent indifference to the plight of suffering humanity in Central Africa. Did God really care? Doubting the goodness of God is not the same as adultery and murder. Nevertheless, it is sin.

People are different, and circumstances are different. But we are alike in that we all fail, and we fail for the same basic reason: we are still sinners. It's as simple as that. But that is not the last word on the subject.

By itself, the statement that we are still sinful could be misleading; it could be twisted to suggest that since we are still sinners, it's okay to be complacent about sin. Such is not the case. The New Testament is completely hostile to the notion that believers may sin casually or with reckless abandon. In a paragraph that sets forth New Testament standards of behavior appropriate among believers, Peter said, "Be self-controlled. . . . As obedient children, do not conform to the evil desires you had when you lived in ignorance. But just as he who called you is holy, so be holy in all you do; for it is written: 'Be holy, because I am holy'" (1 Peter 1:13–16).

In the same chapter, Peter speaks of the "sanctifying work of the Spirit, for obedience to Jesus Christ" (v. 2). The dictionary tells us that the verb "to sanctify" means "to set apart to a sacred office or to religious use or observance; to hallow." The dictionary's definition agrees with the Bible's use of the word. In the Bible, the root idea of the word "to sanctify" is to set apart.

The word *hallow* is related to the word *holy*, and no basic difference exists between "holy" and "sanctified" or "to make holy" and "to sanctify." "Sanctify" and its related forms come to us through Latin, whereas "holy" and its related forms come from the Anglo-Saxon language. Thus, Peter could just as easily have said, "Live sanctified lives."

Sanctification is a complex subject in the Bible. It is also important, as indicated by Paul's simple but forceful statement, "It is God's will that you should be sanctified [holy]" (1 Thessalonians 4:3). God wants His people to be holy, and He intends to make us holy. Meanwhile, He has not left us on our own but has claimed us for Himself.

That is what sanctification means. God claims us as His own. The moment we trusted Christ, we were sanctified; we were set apart for God as distinct from the rest of the world. This is that aspect of sanctification commonly referred to as *positional* sanctification. A second aspect of sanctification is *practical* or *progressive* sanctification. We'll look at each of these aspects.

POSITIONAL SANCTIFICATION

In the Old Testament, persons and things alike were sanctified. Aaron's sons were sanctified, Mount Sinai was sanctified, the tabernacle and the temple were sanctified, and often even houses and fields were sanctified (Exodus 19:22–23; 29:44; Leviticus

27:14–28; Isaiah 8:13; 1 Peter 3:15). Obviously, none of those things were made holy in the sense of moral or spiritual purity. They were called holy because they were set apart for God's purposes and service. A man's house could be set apart for the Lord's use, and the man himself could be set apart for the Lord's use.

In that sense, every Christian is completely sanctified. Whether he is faithful and obedient or not, he has been set apart for God because of his relationship to Jesus Christ. That is what Peter means when he speaks of "the sanctifying work of the Spirit" (1 Peter 1:2).

Two other texts highlight the same truth. First, Hebrews 10:14 says that "by one sacrifice he [the Lord] has *made perfect forever* those who are being made holy" (emphasis added). Second, Paul described the Christians in Corinth as "the church of God in Corinth . . . those *sanctified in Christ Jesus* and called to be holy" (1 Corinthians 1:2).

Because we are *in* Christ, we are sanctified. Our relationship to Christ constitutes our sanctification. Because we are in Him, and because being in Him gives us acceptance before God, we are set apart for God *by God*—which is the meaning of positional sanctification.

PRACTICAL SANCTIFICATION

The two texts just mentioned also allude to the second aspect of sanctification—the practical or progressive. The idea is conveyed in the phrase "called to be holy." "Sanctified" and "called to be holy" represent positional and progressive sanctification respectively. Since we are set apart for God, we are called to live godly lives. We are called to *practice* holy living, to be actively engaged in doing the things that please God.

Christians living in Corinth had failed miserably to live godly lives, as Paul reminded them in his first letter to them. They were still living sinfully. Yet Paul addressed them as "sanctified in Christ Jesus." By virtue of their relationship to Christ, they were sanctified. But they were not practicing godliness; they were not living as sanctified people. Paul's letter rebuked them and reminded them that they were called to live out their positional sanctification in practical obedience to God.

The practical (i.e., not theoretical but lived out in action) aspect of sanctification relates to the manner of living appropriate for those whom God claims as His own. It isn't easy to live consistently as a person set apart to God. That's why we have the warnings and exhortations in the New Testament for us to shape up as Christians. Paul says in Romans 6:19 and 22,

Just as you used to offer the parts of your body in slavery to impurity and to ever-increasing wickedness, so now offer them in slavery to righteousness leading to holiness . . . But now that you have been set free from sin and have become slaves to God, the benefit you reap leads to holiness, and the result is eternal life.

God gets down to basic essentials. The kind of sanctification He requires is extremely practical. Consequently, sanctified people are not those with their heads in the clouds; they are those who know the difference between evil and good and seek, with God's help, to avoid evil and do good.

Practical Sanctification Is Progressive

God, by His Holy Spirit, positionally sanctifies us—completely and instantaneously—when we receive Jesus Christ as Savior. Practical sanctification, on the other hand, is a continuous process as long as we are on earth. God expects us to progress in our growing in Christ and obeying Him—through the power of the Holy Spirit dwelling in us. We are called to "make every effort to live in peace with all men and to be holy; without holiness no one will see the Lord" (Hebrews 12:14). All of us have a long way to go. John Bunyan did not title his book *The Pilgrim's Progress* merely because he believed it was an attractive title. Striving to be more and more like Christ over the course of a lifetime is the essence of Christian living.

Ironically, however, the holier a person becomes, the less conscious he or she may be of spiritual growth. On the one hand, he knows he no longer loses his temper as he did when he was a new Christian. The closer his walk with God, however, the more aware he becomes of God's perfections and his own imperfections, so that he cannot "pat himself on the back" for having learned to control his temper. Instead, he mourns over inadequacies of which he alone may be conscious.

Unfortunately, it is possible for a genuine Christian *not* to make progress and to be unaware of her or his spiritual stagnation. In at least two New Testament Epistles, believers are rebuked for spiritual shallowness. The Christians in Corinth were pathetically worldly and immature. Paul called them spiritual infants (1 Corinthians 3:1). The believers to whom Hebrews was addressed were also immature. The writer said they needed milk, not solid food, and he suspected them of being lazy (Hebrews 5:11–6:2, 12).

Renewal of the mind is part of the sanctifying process, as is clear from various texts. Paul wrote, "Do not conform any longer to the pattern of this world, but be transformed by the renewing of your mind" (Romans 12:2). In another place Paul wrote, "You have taken off your old self with its practices and have put on the new self, which is being renewed in knowledge in the image of its Creator" (Colossians 3:9–10).

Restoration. For sins committed *before* conversion, we need forgiveness and salvation. For sins committed after conversion, we need forgiveness and restoration. David felt the need for restoration to God, and he rejoiced in its possession. "When I kept silent [about my sin]," he said, "my bones wasted away through my groaning all day long" (Psalm 32:3). Then David turned to the Lord in prayer and confession: "Then I acknowledged my sin to you and did not cover up my iniquity. I said, 'I will confess my transgressions to the Lord'" (v. 5).

What happened next? The Lord "forgave the guilt of [his] sin," so that David could exult in the knowledge that God did not hold his sins against him. With forgiveness comes restoration. Later, David wrote the Twenty-third Psalm, which includes the missionary Fred Stanley Arnot's favorite verse: "He restoreth my soul."

Restoration is part of the sanctifying process. All of us fail many times. We need frequent forgiveness, and we need restoration. The good news is that God restores our souls. He gives us the spiritual lift we need. Moreover, He dusts us off; He cleanses us. When John says in 1 John 1:9, "If we confess our sins, he is faithful and just and will forgive us our sins and purify us from all unrighteousness," he echoes David.

In Psalm 23:3 David says that the Lord both restores his soul *and* guides him in paths of righteousness "for his name's sake." For the sake of the Lord's name? Yes! God has a stake in His children. What is His initial sanctifying work if not His claiming us for Himself? He has a stake in us, and He will not discard us. When we come confessing our sins, He restores us, cleanses us, and shows us how to do what is right.

Death to sin. Paul says in Romans 6:2, "We died to sin," then immediately asks, "How can we live in it any longer?" In verse 6 he says that "our old self was crucified with him [Christ]." Paul does not set forth death to sin as a process but as an accomplished fact. "We *died* to sin," and "our old self *was* crucified." The tenses help us understand Paul's meaning. Furthermore, in statements at the end of the paragraph, Paul makes clear that his use of the death metaphor is not intended to indicate a process but an accomplished act. "The death he [Christ] died, he died to sin once for all; but the life he lives, he lives to God. In the same way, count yourselves dead to sin but alive to God in Christ Jesus" (Romans 6:10–11).

Since Christ had no sinful inclinations, what does Paul mean in saying that Christ died to sin? Christ's death to sin was His death on the cross. At no time did Christ personally sin. His "death to sin" was His bearing sin's penalty for us at Calvary. Sin demands the death of every sinner. In accepting responsibility for the sins of humankind, Christ made Himself vulnerable to death. He also had to die. But by dying, He satisfied sin's claims; sin now has no claim on Him. He doesn't have to die again. That is the meaning of the expression that He "died to sin once for all."

That is also the meaning of *our* death to sin. Although we are not literally dead, nevertheless in Christ we have died to sin. What Christ accomplished on the cross is credited to our account, so that God views us as having paid sin's penalty—death. "One [Christ] died for all, and therefore all died [in Him]" (2 Corinthians 5:14).

It is comforting to know that whatever claims sin had on us were taken care of at Calvary. Christ died to sin by suffering and dying on the cross, and He did it once for all. We also died to sin once for all, not by experiencing literal death but by becoming, through faith, part of Him. We are *in Christ*, and *in Him* we died to sin once for all.

Our standing vs. our state. Regarding our being "dead to sin," we are talking about a legal standing before God. Being able to respond to sin is not the issue in Romans 6, in which the expressions "dead to sin" and "alive to God" occur (v. 11). The issue is our standing before God, not our spiritual state. Many Christians, failing to understand that, believe that this passage teaches that Christians are no longer able to respond to sin. Yet they know they *can*.

They feel the force of temptation and, as does everyone else, often fall into sin of some kind. They become miserable in their striving to attain what can never be attained—a life free of temptation and sin. They begin to question the reality of their relationship with God. They fear that they were never born again, or, having been saved, became unsaved.

"Dead to sin" does not mean immunity to temptation and sinful actions. The old, sinful nature will not die until our bodies die. Not until we expire will we cease to feel the force of temptation. But God tells us to *reckon* (i.e., to count) ourselves to be dead to sin and alive to God in Christ Jesus. He tells us to live as *if* sin had no claim on us and no power in our lives. That's not easy to do, but by God's help and with practice and self-discipline, it becomes easier. As someone once said, "We cannot be sinless, but we can sin less."

That is essentially the gist of Paul's exhortation in Colossians 3:5, 8–10:

> *Put to death, therefore, whatever belongs to your earthly nature: sexual immorality, impurity, lust, evil desires and greed, which is idolatry . . . You must rid yourselves of all such things as these: anger, rage, malice, slander, and filthy language from your lips. Do not lie to each other, since you have taken off your old self with its practices and have put on the new self, which is being renewed in knowledge in the image of its Creator.*

God wants us to be different from what we were when we were first saved. He wants us to lay aside evil habits and to form new habits that are appropriate in those whom God calls to His kingdom and glory. Developing a new self is a lifelong process. If you haven't made much progress, don't be discouraged. Don't conclude that you were never saved. Instead, seek anew the help of the Sanctifier, the Holy Spirit of God.

SUMMARY

$\mathcal{T}$he primary benefits of salvation are the irreversible things that God does for us. He forgives us; He redeems us; He justifies us; He reconciles us to Himself; He adopts us; and He sanctifies us. Each of these magnificent verbs describes an action by God—and also a new relationship that we have with Him. Yet we cannot *feel* these primary benefits in the usual sense of the word. We don't *feel* justified. We don't *feel* reconciled.

Other secondary benefits of salvation we may experience more directly and consciously. We can feel them. These are secondary in the sense that they flow from the primary benefits. A person who is not justified is lost. But a justified person may go through life without assurance of salvation. It is crucial that he be justified; it is less important that he know it. However, if he knows he is saved, he can *feel* the secondary benefits of salvation, including the joy of assurance. God wants us to enjoy being saved. That's why Paul prayed, "May the God of hope fill you with all joy and peace as you trust in him, so that you may overflow with hope by the power of the Holy Spirit" (Romans 15:13).

Many saved people are not sure they are saved. They *hope* they are saved, but they do not *know* they are saved, even though they have done everything God asks them to do to receive His gift of salvation. Some Christians are anxious and filled with foreboding. One day they will realize in heaven that their anxiety on earth about salvation was unnecessary and unhelpful.

> *Some think so, they hope so, they trust so, they guess so,*
> *But I know, I know I am saved,*
> *For I've opened my heart's door, and Christ has come in,*
> *And I know that He saves me, and keeps me from sin.*
> *Some think so, they hope so, they trust so, they guess so,*
> *But I know, I know I am saved.*
>
> —EVEREK R. STORMS

Assurance is certainty, and certainty is crucial to peace of mind and persistence in the face of adversity. If we did not have some assurance that we would reach our heavenly destination in spite of many failures in this life, we would probably give up. That, of course, is what many Christians do. But believers who are assured of salvation are positive they will get to heaven. They do not just *hope* they are saved; they *know* they are saved.

On the other hand, many genuine Christians believe that it is presumptuous to be assured of salvation. As we have seen repeatedly, however, the Bible gives ample reason for a believer in Jesus

Christ to have complete confidence that he or she is saved.

A distinction should be made between security and assurance. Some persons may be brimming with assurance, confident that they are on the way to heaven, when in fact they are on the road to hell. Their hope is false assurance, based on something other than the grace of God. This booklet is not written for them. It is written for deeply sincere believers who, having believed the gospel, are eternally secure, yet have no assurance that they are in fact safe and secure.

Security, or eternal security, denotes the doctrine that salvation is irrevocable; it is permanent. Eternal security is the doctrine alluded to by the expression "once saved, always saved." If that doctrine is biblical and therefore true, a saved person may have the assurance that he or she is eternally secure. She can *know* that she is saved forever.

Scripture does indeed teach the doctrine of eternal security. It teaches this great truth in at least three ways: by the use of terms that require permanence, by direct statements affirming the truth of eternal security, and by powerful implications.

TERMS THAT REQUIRE PERMANENCE

The New Testament makes at least thirty references to eternal life. Among these are two familiar texts:

Just as Moses lifted up the snake in the desert, so the Son of Man must be lifted up, that everyone who believes in him may have eternal life. (John 3:14–15)

For the wages of sin is death, but the gift of God is eternal life in Christ Jesus our Lord. (Romans 6:23)

The point of those texts is obvious: the life offered to believers in Jesus is *eternal*. This greatest and most undeserved blessing of God, given to every person who believes in His Son, is everlasting life. The gospel does not offer only temporary benefits; it offers *eternal* life. If the gift could be withdrawn for any reason, it would not be eternal. If it could be lost, the phrase "eternal life," which the Bible uses so frequently, would be inaccurate and inappropriate.

Not every Christian is reassured by the word *eternal*. Some believers agree that the gift is eternal life but contend that it is granted conditionally. Unless a person possesses the gift at the moment of death, they argue, he does not enter into eternal life— no matter how long he may have possessed the gift before that time. But it is not God's character to grant salvation and then, at the end, snatch it away!

ETERNAL SECURITY IS
TAUGHT BY DIRECT STATEMENTS

God's Word gives direct statements guaranteeing the permanence of our salvation. Jesus said, "I tell you the truth, whoever hears my word and believes him who sent me has eternal life and will not be condemned; he has crossed over from death to life" (John 5:24). He also said, "My sheep listen to my voice; I know them, and they follow me. I give them eternal life, and they shall never perish; no one can snatch them out of my hand" (John 10:27–28).

Both of these statements by Jesus not only speak of eternal life (life that cannot end), they also emphasize the point by saying in the first passage that those who believe "*will not* be condemned" and by saying in the second passage that "they *shall never* perish" and that "*no one* can snatch them out of [the Lord's] hand."

Paul was convinced "that neither death nor life, neither angels nor demons, neither the present nor the future, nor any powers, neither height nor depth, nor anything else in all creation, will be able to separate us from the love of God that is in Christ Jesus our Lord" (Romans 8:38–39).

The apostle ruled out every possibility—angelic and demonic, heavenly and earthly, present or future—of a believer's ever losing the gift of life he has in Christ. You are eternally secure, Paul implied in a letter to believers in Philippi, because "he who began a good work in you will carry it on to completion until the day of Christ Jesus" (Philippians 1:6).

The importance of these texts can hardly be exaggerated. Nothing can separate us from the love of God. Having begun a work in us, God will continue it until the work is done. He is committed to our salvation. God will no more let us go than He will let His own Son go, because we are now *in* His Son. "Once saved, always saved" is not a wishful cliché. It is a glorious truth.

Salvation, once granted, is permanent. It is an irrevocable gift. God promises us that He will not take it from us and that nothing else and no one else can take it from us. Christ is "able to save *forever* those who draw near to God through Him, since He always lives to make intercession for them" (Hebrews 7:25 NASB, emphasis added).

ETERNAL SECURITY IS
TAUGHT BY IMPLICATION

The Bible's use of the phrase "eternal life" and its many direct statements affirming the irrevocability of salvation should be enough to reassure anxious people. But God gives still further evidence in His Word that you can know you are saved forever. The strongest argument in support of eternal security is the nature of salvation itself.

That has been the message of this booklet—that eternal security is inseparable from the nature of salvation. Salvation is not just a gift; it is a state of being that cannot be altered. It is a fixed standing before God that He Himself creates and legislates into existence when a person believes the gospel.

When a person believes the gospel, irreversible things happen. What happens is irreversible, because it is *God's* doing. *God* forgives; *God* redeems; *God* justifies; *God* reconciles; *God* adopts; *God* sanctifies; and *God* does whatever else may be necessary to round out our salvation.

What happens is irreversible because it introduces a new state of being. As Jesus said, "I tell you the truth, whoever hears my word and believes him who sent me has eternal life and will not be condemned; he has crossed over from death to life" (John 5:24).

That powerful promise's use of the present tense ("*has* eternal life") indicates that eternal life is received immediately upon believing. Its reference to crossing from death to life indicates the irrevocability of the gift. When God gives eternal life, something wonderful happens to the believer: he receives eternal life, and he passes from one standing to another. He no longer stands under God's judgment; he has crossed from death to life.

Paul echoes Jesus' words in various places. Consider Colossians 1:13–14. Speaking of the Father's work in saving us, Paul said, "He has rescued us from the dominion of darkness and brought us into the kingdom of the Son he loves, in whom we have redemption, the forgiveness of sins."

We have crossed over from death to life, and we have been delivered from the kingdom of darkness and brought into the kingdom of God's beloved Son. This new standing before God is irreversible. Furthermore, it is attested to by the gift of the Holy Spirit. After telling new believers that they had been included in Christ, Paul explains how it happened: "Having believed, you were marked in him with a seal, the promised Holy Spirit, who is a deposit guaranteeing our inheritance until the redemption of those who are God's possession—to the praise of his glory" (Ephesians 1:13–14).

Here, then, is powerful proof that every true believer is eternally secure. Salvation is God's work from start to finish. All we can do is repent and believe the gospel. When we believe, we are included in Christ. We are marked with a seal, God's Holy Spirit. The Holy Spirit in us is a God-given guarantee that we will receive everything God has promised. The Holy Spirit is also evidence that we *now* belong to God, that we are His possession. In that great truth we *are* secure, and we should *feel* secure. God will not let anyone or anything steal His beloved children.

If you have believed the gospel and, therefore, have opened your heart to Jesus, you are eternally secure. But you can *know* that you are saved only to the extent that you know and understand the Scriptures and believe them. God saves you when you believe in Jesus, and He wants you to know it. That is what the apostle John tells us when he says in 1 John 5:11–13, "God has given us eternal life, and this life is in his Son. He who has the Son has life; he who does not have the Son of God does not have life. I write these things to you who believe in the name of the Son of God *so that you may know* that you have eternal life" (emphasis added).

If you still don't know whether you are saved or not, is it because you are unwilling to be reassured? God has said everything needed to reassure you. You can *know* that you are eternally saved and rejoice in the fact. Choose then to believe God, and enter into the joy of your salvation.

————————❧❧————————

Examining
CONTROVERSIAL TEXTS

Some texts seem to teach that believers can lose their salvation. Curiously, not all believers feel troubled by the possibility that they could be saved and then lost again. They may even vigorously defend that belief, as if they derived comfort from it. But most Christians are sincerely troubled by such texts, and for their sakes the following comments on texts most frequently cited may be helpful.

THE IMPORTANCE OF THE CONTEXT

First, troublesome texts are usually given meanings their respective contexts do not permit. For example, Jesus' statement that "he who stands firm to the end will be saved" comes in the context of teaching about the future, specifically the Great Tribulation (Matthew 10:22; 24:13; Mark 13:13). In that context, it becomes clear that "he who stands firm to the end" refers to all who, living in that terrible time that is yet to come, refuse the mark of the Beast (Revelation 14:9–12).

True believers of *all* times do indeed stand firm, as is evident from passages like Romans 14:4 and Jude 24. Jude praises "him who is able to keep [us] from falling and to present [us] before his glorious presence without fault and with great joy." God does not keep us from sinning; He does, however, keep us from falling away and thus losing our salvation.

FREQUENTLY CITED (AND MISUNDERSTOOD) TEXTS

1. Matthew 5:13—"If the salt loses its saltiness, how can it be made salty again? It is no longer good for anything, except to be thrown out and trampled by men." Pure salt (sodium chloride) cannot lose its saltiness, but it can become contaminated to the point where it is useless. In ancient Palestine, contaminated salt was thrown out.

Like contaminated salt, Christians can be spoiled by the world and lose their effectiveness for God. Paul warns against this in Colossians 2:8. Peter describes believers who fail to grow in grace in 2 Peter 1:9. They give off the flavor of contaminants. But unlike useless, contaminated salt, they are not thrown out. They are still precious in God's sight.

2. Matthew 12:32—"Anyone who speaks against the Holy Spirit will not be forgiven, either in this age or in the age to come." This is the unpardonable sin. It troubles many who, having uttered blasphemous things, fear that they are forever doomed. Included

in this group are conscientious believers who, questioning the validity of somebody else's claim to speak or act for God, were told they had blasphemed the Holy Spirit. Hence their anxiety about loss of salvation.

The sin in question is "*the* blasphemy against the Spirit" (v. 31, emphasis added). Note the article *the*. It indicates a particular kind of blasphemy. The context reveals what it is: the ascribing of the source of Jesus' power to the Devil rather than to the Holy Spirit. The men who committed the sin had seen Jesus' work. He had healed a demon-possessed man before their eyes. So their sin of saying that He did it under the power and authority of Satan was willful rejection of the Lord, whom they knew to be filled with the Holy Spirit. Their contemptuous charge reflected an attitude of *fixed* opposition to Him. No true believer is capable of a sin even remotely similar to that.

3. John 15:6—"If anyone does not remain in me, he is like a branch that is thrown away and withers; such branches are picked up, thrown into the fire and burned." This is an apparent allusion to Judas Iscariot, the supreme example of apostasy. Just before the discourse of which this text is part, Judas was ordered out of the room where the Lord met with His disciples. Judas was never a believer, as is evident from John 6:70. Jesus said he was a devil. No true believer can commit apostasy. True believers remain in Christ.

4. 1 Timothy 4:1—"In later times some will abandon the faith and follow deceiving spirits and things taught by demons." It's clear that Paul was thinking of apostates, not true believers. In

verse 3, apostates are contrasted with "those who believe and who know the truth." Apostates are those who, John said, "went out from us, but they did not really belong to us. For if they had belonged to us, they would have remained with us; but their going showed that none of them belonged to us" (1 John 2:19).

In the very next verse, John tells true believers that they have "an anointing from the Holy One, and all of you know the truth." True believers do not follow doctrines of demons. It should be clear that Paul's warning about apostasy is not directed at true believers.

5. Hebrews 6:4–6—"It is impossible for those who have once been enlightened . . . if they fall away, to be brought back to repentance, because to their loss they are crucifying the Son of God all over again."

This passage is cited frequently by Christians who fear that, having backslidden, they have lost their salvation. But if that is what it means, it says more than anyone is willing to accept—that a single instance of backsliding is fatal; a backslider can never repent and be saved again. That notion is contrary to cherished beliefs, such as God's readiness to receive a repentant prodigal son (Luke 15:11–24; cf. Hosea 14).

The passage is troublesome because it *seems* to describe true believers. It is concerned with those who have been "enlightened," who have "tasted the heavenly gift," and so on. Yet any and all of those descriptive phrases could be true of an unbeliever. Judas is a prime example of one who shared the benefits of the company of Jesus. Judas probably cast out demons in Christ's name, as did the other disciples (Luke 10:20). And in the early days of the gospel, thousands of people were swept into the church. Doubtless many were not truly converted, and when persecution arose, they showed their true colors, falling away (1 John 2:19).

It's important to see that they did not fall into sin; they fell away. Hence, they were not mere backsliders; they were apostates who said, in effect, that Jesus should have been crucified. They were crucifying Him all over again. The passage doesn't deal with mere backsliders, as the term is commonly used; it deals with apostates and warns that deliberate, final rejection of Christ is fatal.

6. Hebrews 10:26–27—"If we deliberately keep on sinning after we have received the knowledge of the truth, no sacrifice for sins is left, but only a fearful expectation of judgment." The subjects of this passage are the same as those contemplated in Hebrews 6:4–6. They are described as "enemies of God" (v. 27), who have "trampled the Son of God under foot" (v. 29). They have "insulted the Spirit of grace" (v. 29). Clearly, they are not backsliders; they are not true believers who burn out and leave the church. Rather, they are apostates who have rejected the sacrifice of Christ, of which the writer speaks so beautifully in Hebrews 10. That is their sin, and the writer tells them that no other sacrifice will save them. Instead, judgment awaits them.

OBJECTIVE TRUTHS VS.
SUBJECTIVE TESTS OF FAITH

Believers who depend on their current spiritual state for assurance will probably seesaw between joy and despair. The saintliest believer is not always conscious of the Lord's presence; as does everybody else, he or she also has spiritual ups and downs. If assurance depends on *feeling* saved, many believers will feel unsaved part of the time. Assurance must rest on objective truths, namely those that set forth God's work on our behalf.

One activity that can keep conscientious believers from having the assurance they need is to subject themselves to a self-evaluation test such as: "Do I love God and hate the world?" "Do I sense the inner workings of the Holy Spirit?" "Do I keep God's commandments?" Sensitive believers continually question the depth of their love for God, the quality of their obedience, and so on. If they depend on their own, often anguished, answers to questions such as these, they will despair of ever knowing for certain that they are truly saved.

True, the apostle John uses certain expressions like "if we say . . ." and "by this we know . . ." that are clearly designed to test the validity of a claim to know God. But the point of his tests is to reassure true believers who were being told that they weren't saved *and* to expose false teachers who said that holiness was unimportant and that Christians could do anything they felt like doing. In response, John said that "he who does what is right is righteous. . . . He who does what is sinful is of the devil" (1 John 3:7–8). John's strong language in his first epistle is calculated to reassure believers. False people, on the other hand, are clearly exposed. *They* never ask themselves whether they love God and keep His commandments.

Every true believer *knows* that he believes in Jesus. As John said, "Anyone who believes in the Son of God has this testimony in his heart" (1 John 5:10). To all who have believed in the Son of God, John said, "I write these things . . . so that you may know that you have eternal life" (1 John 5:13).

A FINAL WORD

Luke remembered Berea with affection and respect. The Bereans, he said, "received the message with great eagerness and examined the Scriptures every day to see if what Paul said was true" (Acts 17:11).

My prayer for you is that you also will have read this with eagerness and will examine the Scriptures carefully to see if this message is true. If the position taken here is sound, it will bear up under the tests of Scripture.

As for those to whom this is dedicated, I can say with the apostle Paul, "I thank my God every time I remember you. . . . Being confident of this, that he who began a good work in you will carry it on to completion until the day of Christ Jesus" (Philippians 1:3, 6).

May the Lord give you also the same confidence. There is no greater source of joy than assurance of salvation and no greater incentive to holy living than the conviction that the gifts and calling of God are irrevocable.

C. Donald Cole, Radio Pastor of the Moody Bible Institute, ministers to multitudes each week through the facilities of the Moody Broadcasting Network (MBN).

One of MBN's more popular programs is *Open Line*, which was hosted by Pastor Cole for many years on Monday and Thursday evenings. He was the featured host on the program's predecessor, *Dial the Pastor*, on WMBI. Pastor Cole has a rich history of radio, including the program *What Do You Say?* when he had an opportunity to respond on the air with solid biblical answers to a variety of questions. He provided verse-by-verse studies of the Bible on *The Living Word*, and was joined by his wife, Naomi, during the last five years of its recorded run. He was ahead of his time offering a Christian viewpoint on current events and issues with "Christian Perspectives on the News" as well as the five-minute "Perspectives." Now on Friday mornings over the Moody Broadcasting Network he does a short commentary on the news from a biblical perspective; these commentaries are available online. He continues to answer questions for MBI's monthly devotional, *Today in the Word*.

Before joining Moody Bible Institute in 1971, Pastor Cole and Naomi served the Lord as missionaries in Angola from 1948 until 1966. Pastor Cole then served as a faculty member of Emmaus Bible College of Dubuque (at that time in Oak Park, IL) and as editor of *Interest* magazine, published by Stewards Foundation, at that time in Wheaton, IL.

The Coles' children are Stephanie, Paul, Andrew, Olga, and Gina. They have thirteen grandchildren, including one in heaven, and two great-grandchildren.

The National Religious Broadcasters Hall of Fame stands as a witness for current communicators, a showcase of warriors for Christ who live exemplary lives of valor and compassion, blazing trails and leaving paths for succeeding generations to follow. NRB's most prestigious award is presented to an individual for invaluable contribution to the field of Christian communications, exhibition of the highest standards, and evidence of faithfulness in Christ. In 2006, Don Cole was inducted into the NRB Hall of Fame. In 1998, he won the NRB Distinguished Service Award.

In 1987, Moody Bible Institute began publishing a new devotional magazine, *Today in the Word*. Since then, editors, writers, and even MBI presidents have come and gone, and only one of the original columnists has remained involved with *Today in the Word* since the beginning: Donald Cole. His column, "Q & A," was included in the original *Today in the Word* issue as a way to supplement the monthly Bible studies with responses to the particular concerns of readers. With humor, clarity, faithfulness to the teaching of Scripture, and his own inimitable voice, Pastor Cole has addressed questions from the complex to the childlike for over twenty years. Readers often comment that they always read "Q & A" first when they get a new *Today in the Word*, and certainly Pastor Cole has left a delightful, distinctive signature on each issue. At age eighty-five, he has no intention of retiring from writing "Q & A," and all of us at *Today in the Word*—editors and readers alike—are thankful!

Heather Moffitt
Managing Editor
Today in the Word
Moody Bible Institute